Paintings of the Imagination

Doris J. McGohon

PublishAmerica
Baltimore

First printing

At the specific preference of the author, PublishAmerica allowed this work to remain exactly as the author intended, verbatim, without editorial input.

ISBN: 1-4241-5764-1
PUBLISHED BY PUBLISHAMERICA, LLLP
www.publishamerica.com
Baltimore

Printed in the United States of America

A Gift for Him, A Gift for Me

What gift,can I, to the Lord bring,
When riches are His treasure?
Give my heart without measure
Unto the king of all Kings"!

Now I sit robed in white
A child of light, I am.
Glory to God in the highest
For the eternal gift of the Lamb!

A Lady

She poses quite serenly.
in lovely attire
Long flowing hair is carefully
fashioned in a bonnet.
She sits in a lovely gossamer gown.
She is a natural beauty.
Hers is one of the hidden
person of the heart,
Keeping clear of ungodliness.
She is a lady.
Her husband has no need
to doubt her fidelity.
Being faithful to his trust-
She responds as his helpmeet.
She is a lady.
She excells in the work
of her home...church,
and In charitable services.
she has no lack.
She is a lady.

A Mighty Hold (Tetractys)

Molds
Too tight
Restricts you
Can't know freedom
Be original and think for yourself.

A Picture of Ireland

The hills painted an emerald green
Setting just above the valley's below,
The sheep grazing on four leaf clovers
At the ege of pristine streams that flow.

Cottages nestled in the countryside
With hollyocks, their gardens, to grace,
Linear guards with flowery faces
Share the garden with Queen Ann's lace.

Such a glorious sight will be Ireland
A land of fantasy, beauty unmatched,
Yes, always one will be attached,
Loving, forever smitten by Ireland.

A Shelter from the Winds

I'd like a little cabin in the wooded countryside,
And face it toward the hill, and with my love abide.

All of us would use the porch, rocking as we'd talk
In our olden rocking chairs, and now and then we'd walk.

We'd go o'er the meadows walking hand in hand,
Enjoying all of nature in this majestic land.

I'd have a little garden and work daily in the soil,
I'd cherish every petal with every ounce of toil.

We'd plant trees all around—willows here and maples there,
A little patch of sunlight, well, maybe over there.

Morning glories would brighten the chimney of our home,
And from our quaint little place we'd never want to roam.

The mighty river would beckon at the foot of the hill,
And yield its bountiful food until we had our fill.

We'd listen to the crickets and watch the fireflys bright,
As we sat in our rockers on a hot summer night.

In the coldness of the winter the fire would feel so good,
Around our cozy fireplace with the cracklin' of the wood.

Our cabin would shelter us on a snowy winter night,
From the mighty howling winds, as we pulled our covers tight.

It reminds me of a shelter our Father has prepared
Through the mighty work of Jesus, for His blood was not spared.

A shelter from the howling winds our God will be to us,
If we'll just receive His Son, as a little child, in trust

A Small Town

There is a charming quality about a small town
Where the living is good
And greeting is pleasant.
A warm expression veils many faces,
While kindliness extends to the stranger.
In the summertime one can hardly wait
For the county fair to commence.
A sense of excitement fills the air,
From the parade, to the contests galore,
To the equine competitions -
All decked out in shining coats,
Prancing with pride and pomposity,
And on to the carnival – while
Young and old scream with delight and fear
As they conquer their demons!
The Mayor sings the favorite
Country ballads with strong emotion,
While one aspires to Nashville.
How satisfied one is to be from a small town!
There is something akin to Mayberry
In this, our small town.

A Storm (Swap Quatrain)

I've weathered many storms of late,
Sought for comfort in this sad state.
My happiness has been tethered
Many storms of late, I've weathered.

Sea billows roll upon the shore,
In anger they're laid up in store,
All dignity the black storm stole,
Upon the shore, sea billows roll.

The clouds, no longer gray and dark.
The storm on me, has left its mark,
They came to console me,the crowds
No longer grey and dark, the clouds.

A Thankful Heart (Etheree)

Troubles are rampant, life throws a lemon,
that's the time to offer thanksgiving
before self enters selfishly.
He screams for his liberty,
wanting only his way
fretting and fumming,
knowing not good
He must die
quickly
now.

Affirmation

Have I ever said, "Thank you,
"You're doing a good job,
"I appreciate you?"
Or were you the one I robbed?

Robbed of the joyful smile
That comes from doing right,
Failing to notice the sadness,
Expressions, that could've been light.

All Encompassing Love

In eternity,
Love was born of a union,
when mercy kissed grace.

Amidst the Wild Flowers

The path was an arduous one
That led up and around the mountain
Where the wild flowers grew
So freely on the mountain.
While walking under the trees
My eyes lit upon a fair maiden,
In a secluded place on the the trail,
Picking a bouquet of red trillium
And small sprigs of sweet William,
Gathering them in a pail.
She was unaware of my presence,
As she was lost in her world.
I never shall forget the time
and the sweet maiden so fair,
Innocent, standing there,
Amidst wildflowers on the mountain.

Another's Problem

The air is so fresh and clean,
With my Lord and me, nothing in between.

Haven't got a problem in the world
With anyone, no, not even a quarrel.

Since I've no problems in my life,
Why do I sometimes feel such strife?

Can it be another's problem becomes my own
Where in secret chambers they must go alone?

Though a burden bearer I'm called to be,
More oft than not it's 'tween God and them.

As You've Done It Unto These

I'll acknowledge you my brother,
And the things you have to say.
I've little advise or other,
But together we could pray.

I'll try hard to listen,
And read between the lines
To see if joy is missing,
And your troubled heart pines.

I hope to build you up,
And never tear you down;
God forbid I'd be abrupt,
And talkativness abound.

We always need each other,
For He declared it so,
And I pledge to you, my brother,
The love of God I'll show.

Autumn

The mountains are ablaze
with brilliant colors
that stagger the senses.
Summer is gone and Autumn
plays her grand finale.

The October sky is crystal clear
with cumulus clouds akin to
fluffy white wool.
The urge to recline there,
if it were possible,
is almost irresistible.

The air turns crisp like
freshly bought celery.
Daylight is brief,
and darkness is a welcome
respite to dream of this
intoxicating time.

The trees gently shed
their leaves of red, and gold
while all nature claps her hands,
and glorifies the Creator!
The apples lay down their bounty
and scent the air with the freshness
of a crisp fall morning.

The squirrels ready
a place to hoard nuts,
while the birds migrate south
to a destination foreordained.

We'll relish some steamy
chili made with hot peppers
these chilly, uncertain,
days of Autumn

A fresh quality of excitement
is in the air, while
Chimneys bellow out their protest
of the soon coming cold.

O' Holy Father, I thank
and praise you for
the beauty of nature this day,
and for all of your provisions.

Available

The lessons I'm learning seem quite severe
As God is stripping me of all veneer.
A mask no longer He'll permit.
I've got to get real bit by bit.

God wants me on an unpretentious level,
Be real with Him and resist the devil.
He has made each one of us so unique,
And we need Him each day of the week.

In our uniqueness He lives His life,
To touch the world and all of it's strife.
We must let Him love the worst of all,
We must treat them tenderly when they fall.

Such great love I must not withhold,
For in sin's slavery I once was sold.
He sought me out and brought me back
In tender mercy, there was no lack.

Lord, here am I, a vessel to use,
It's only me, Lord, but without excuse.
The two of us will be as one
Entering love's battle 'till the victory's won.

Be Still

The days are filled with distractions,
And we must find quietness with our God
Within the clamor of much to do,
A place where feet have never trod.

"Because Of"

Marital love will not survive,
If only you love "because of;"
No, it would scarcely be alive-
This crippled thing called love.

"I love you because of
"The way you make me feel."
But what happens in marriage
When you're no longer thrilled?

When one has lost everything,
Will you keep on walking?
The temptation is quite alluring
Attraction is always stalking.

Commitment is the answer
That will hold a marriage true,
Selfishness will destroy it
Commitment is the glue.

The key to mankind's selfishness
Is love upon a tree.
His arms are opened wide
For sinful man, it's clear to see.

Behold the Lamb

Behold the Lamb
That takes away all sin,
The precious Word of God
Sent down from God to man.

Behold the Lamb
With nail prints in His hand,
And pain upon His face,
As darkness hides the land.

Behold the lamb,
The stone is rolled away,
And down Emmaeus road
The sky's no longer gray.

Behold the Lamb
Encircled by His friends;
See Him beckon Thomas,
And end his doubting sins.

Behold the Lamb
Taken in clouds of day
To stand before our God;
Love pleading as we pray.

Behold the Lamb
For every knee shall bow.
Don't wait 'till it's too late,
Oh, friend, receive him now.

Beware

He is the prince of this new world
His ploys and schemes he has whirled
Upon us, yet to be unfurled.
Beware old world, beware old world.

He will tempt you with unbelief
Coming upon one as a sneak thief
Never giving any relief
Evil is he, evil is he.

My Lord comforted me today
He comforted me along the way
Satan had followed me, the prey
Along the way, along the way.

Billows of the Sea

You had a zest for living
But suddenly you were gone,
Moving to a different sphere
As if you were drawn.

The memory of you left
Waves of grief that o'erflowed me,
As sea billows churning,
gales to the meadow to flee.

By the Sea (Quatern)

The old man who lived by the sea
Once accosted the likes of me
He was a beachcomber at heart,
But he had wisdom to impart.

Not knowing him I thought to flee…
The old man who lived by the sea.
But his kind eyes beckoned me there
For to hear of his lady fair.

It was many years ago now
To him, this fair maid made a vow,
The old man who lived by the sea
loved her with his affection, free.

He told me to love with my heart
For someday you will have to part
Oh, how real was the ernest plea…
The old man who lived by the sea.

Christmas (Acrostic)

Come let us go and find
Him who was born of a virgin,
Royalty lay wrapped up
In swadling clothes in a manger,
Sweet little baby so still
To save the world from sin.
Myrh, frankincense, and gold,
All fit for a King, were the gifts
Savour divine, is He!

Christmas Time

Christmas time is here again,
That wonderous time of the year.
Bringing visions of peace.
Places far and near.

Good tidings of great joy,
Coming to all on Christmas day.
A little child royally lay,
Majesty wrapped up in a boy.

Whoever would have guessed
that He, in all of His splendor,
Would be born in a lowly stable,
This One who was so tender.

But His Father's plan for Him
was in great love decreed.
He would bridge the great chasm
'tween God and the deceived.

.

His Father gave Him up
That He might hang on a tree
For the sins of mankind,
It was in death, He set them free..

May I never get so busy
That I won't stop and be grateful
For His sacrificial death for me
On that decreed day, so fateful.

Come Fly Away With Me

Come fly away with me
To a land of pure delight
To a land where all is bright,
And there'll be no need for the night.

Come fly away with me
To a land where all is life,
Where there'll be no strife,
And mercy and goodness are rife.

Come fly away with me
Where the streets are pure gold
As all men have been told;
And kindness reigns within the fold.

Come fly away with me
Where our saviour abides,
And it's He who decides
Which men He divides -
And bids some to come inside.

Complete

In the silence of the night I feel
His warm love enfolding me.
I dare not move for the moment is holy.
He blankets His love around me,
Holding me close to His heart.
He whispers ever so sweetly of His
Tenderness toward me.
His loving eyes draw me even closer
Until one day our union is complete.
There I will live forever with
The Lover of my soul- Jesus!

Dancing to the Music of Life

I can see it in her eyes,
the sadness of a broken spirit.
Where has her lover gone?
Was he ever there or was that
a figment of her imagination?
He has forgotten the loving eyes
that are now filled with sadness.
She will rise to love again
as a phoenix rises from the ashes.
There is a special one who
will not only show her love,
but will stay with her through
the good and the bad times,
dancing to the music of life as one.

Day of Grace

The hour is fast approaching
When grace shall be no more
Many fates will have been sealed
And closed will be the door.

Enter in while there is time
O' will you not come today?
Be among the ransomed
Before it is too late!

Call upon Jesus to save you
Your sins shall be whiter than snow,
And when all of life is over,
You will reap what Jesus sowed.

Eternal life with God and
All godly ones of the ages,
For you will not be among those
Who receive their own wages.

Death's Last Stand

Bury me deep in the ground,
'Till resurrection, I'll be bound.

My spirit leaves for that fair land,
For to meet the heavn'ly band.

This awsome celebration,
To see Him—anticipation!

Such heavenly music
Thrilling me, so exquisite!

The opulent streets of gold
Are like we were told.

The lush and flowering grounds
Where delicious fruit abounds.

I see the splendid mansions
There are yet expansions.

All people of heaven
Are happy in this haven.

No disease ever again…
Death can't touch me in this land.

Loved ones, all gathered here
By the crystal sea, clear.

Sin is gone forevermore
On heaven's golden shore.

Such a celebration
Is my coronation.

My crowns, I gladly lay
At His feet this heav'nly day.

Dear ones, weep not for me
For soon, my face, you'll see.

Rejoice that we'll meet once again
In heaven, this fair land.

Dreams Of Paradise (Reggae Song)

The white beaches of paradise
Beckon me across the miles.
The dreams of far away places,
Are calling me to the isles.

Palm trees swaying to the music,
Of salty ocean breezes,
A walk along the beach
Is just the thing that pleases.

Chorus
Yes, I hear it plainly now
The beaches are beckoning me
Come to the isles, they say
Mesmerizing me with the sea..

A cacophony of sea gulls
Swoop down into waves of the sea,
Then quickly flying off,
Assuring their fish will not flee.

The sleek body of the dolphin
Dives, and rises up again,
With sharp piercing squeals,
In the sea, his domain.

Chorus
Yes, I hear it plainly now
The beaches are beckoning me
Come to the isles, they say
Mesmerizing me with the sea..

Surfers ride on their shiny boards,
Conquering the mighty waves.
What a thrill watching them
As the growing crowd raves.

I'll search along the shore
For many treasures to find
Perhaps I'll find a pearl in a shell,
One of the finest kind.

Chorus
Yes, I hear it plainly now
The beaches are beckoning me
Come to the isles, they say
Mesmerizing me with the sea..

The white beaches of paradise
Often beckon the child in me,
With thrill of far away places
Where dreams come true by the sea.

Chorus
Yes, I hear it plainly now
The beaches are beckoning me
Come to the isles, they say
Mesmerizing me with the sea..

Echo Through the Ages

Long ago children passed through fire
sacrificed to pagan gods.
The crowds frenzy drowned conscience,
As their screams echoed though the ages.

Wretched demons gorge on victory –
In confidence, they speak,
"These humans always do our bidding."
Their words echoed through the ages.

"They were pagans," we say.
We cringe at their savagery,
their depraved, brutish, and Godless ways.
All the while wretched demons gorge on victory.

"These humans always do our bidding;
Remember Roe V. Wade?"

Except for Her God

Her demeanor was one of confidence
As she applied her makeup ever so carefully.
She was as beautiful as we had hoped,
And our dreams were to be fulfilled
In this girl of "soon to be eighteen."
So much time and preparation
Had been invested in her
But she was worth it!
She was quickly becoming a woman,
Who stands alone in this world,
Except for her God.
Today she paid a visit to her therapist
Who told her what she already knew!

Figment of Imagation

At dusk the clouds
in the distance-
purple and blue hues-
high above the valley-
Enrapture my senses!
Seeping into the
the figment of my imagination-
not seen-
are mountains, quite magnificent.
The mountains I have created-
in inventiveness-
will regrettably disappear
when a new day dawns.

Fleeting Time

The
flower
of her youth
passed quickly by
like a fast moving
train going down the tracks.
Yesterday was a moment
in time that will be remembered.
Some of it will be good and some bad.
Take the good and leave behind the other.

Free As a Bird

Oh, to know freedom!
Free as a bird in flight,
from the prison
of confinement.
school, home and
from various
authority figures.
Freedom to come and go,
at will, whenever
and wherever I please.
No clocks to bother me
and no person to which
an answer is due.
Oh, to be released from these
chains of age!
I'm an adult now, so I'm told,
but sweet freedom without
structure and discipline
is bondage in itself.
Does it elude me still?
In time, I will be
liberated to be a bondslave
of Eternal Love.

Freedom Sounds

The sound of laughter in the air
is a reminder of freedom.
The sound of "The Star Spangled Banner."
is cause to rouse the patriot,
the sound of anxiety in a loved one,
for the one who feels
a patriotic duty to serve,
the sound of lonliness
far away from home,
the sound of bombs exploding,
the sound of wounded comrades,
the sound of loved ones weeping
as sad news has been received,
the sound of pain when
humanity is dying all around,
The sound of "Taps" ring out
for the burial of freedom's warriors,
and the sound of gaiety
that welcomes the hero home,
The sound of love that was their
motive for service.
God bless America's freedom fighters!

God's Grace

God's grace
for life's problems
is the help needed now.
Let the Lord take your hand and lead
you to the victory prepared for you.
Faith is the victory, we're told,
that opens every door
pointing one to
God's grace.

Good Ole Days

Cokes, Sodas, diners, movies,
Turned up collars and poodle skirts,
Were the rage of the fifties crowd;
Changing styles came in spurts.

Sunday dinner of chicken
For the preacher and all,
In that little house of ours
Though the portions were small.

It was a time of great contentment
We were grateful for all we had
Thanking God for all of our bounty,
As the blessing was said by dad.

Oh, what I'd give for the good ole days
When life didn't hurry on.
I'd sit out on the porch swingin'
Until the dusk was dawn.

Hallelujah, Jesus Lives!

Oh, Hallelujah, Jesus lives,
This day your tears begone.
It is a day of victory,
The starting of the dawn.

Oh, Halleujah, Jesus lives,
The scriptures tell us so
There is hope for all mankind
In the precious blood that flows.

Oh, Hallelujah, Jesus lives
To set the sinner free,
And live His life through him
So men of every land might see.

Oh, Halleujah, what a Savior
In the the raging storm He is there
I have no need to fear
For I'm a child of the King, an heir!

Heaven

O' heavenly day when I behold Him
In all of His glory and splendor!
To look into His eyes, in wonder.
Such love, I cannot comprehend.

I'll bow down and worship Him
With tears of joy and anthems of praise,
My hands and heart, I'll raise
Unto Jesus Christ, my King!

It will be heaven enough for me
When I look upon His dear face
To know His rapture and grace
Shall last for all eternity.

Home

Let home be filled with peace and love,
That brightens every nook,
And let it's old pine shelves be full
Of thought provoking books.

Starched, ruffled curtains hung with care
To let the sunshine in,
And don't forget the rocking chair
To go in father's den.

Many pieces full of age
Will dress each happy room,
With window boxes on the sill
In splendor as they bloom.

Thoughts of peace and deeds of love
Will bless this humble place,
As mother tidies up
And puts lilacs in a vase.

Words of welcome grace the door
For the person pausing there.
"Come on in," someone will say,
"Take off your coat, pull up a chair."

May home be such a place, indeed
That weary ones will find
A true refreshment there
Of body, soul, and mind

I Need Your Love

The thrill of loving you
grows stronger with each passing day.
Though time takes it's toll on each of us,
In my eyes you're still the viril,
younthful man that protects and loves me.
When I look into your green eyes,
I see much pain that can only be
healed by God above.
Try as I may, I can only join
my heart to yours and
thank Him for its completion.
Gazing into your eyes,
fastening them upon a sea
of green, I am beckoned
to new heights of love.
I see the strength of the ages,
compassion and kindness.
Within there is unrequited pain.
O' my darling, I love you!
Your strong shoulders and arms
support me in weakness.
I need your love!
The thrill of loving you
grows stronger with each passing day!

I Will Follow You

Like nectar to my lips are your kisses...
They say volumns about you.
Your love is warm and tender
asking nothing in return.
My love, my heart has been affected
by such outpourings.
I am drawn to you as a magnet...
unable to distance myself.
I will follow you no matter what the price
becoming one flesh never to be cut asunder.
I love you so! Let the material things
of this earth pass away...
they will seem as nothing as long as I have you!

Ice Storm

Branches bend and creak
As though with old age.
Black crayola marks paint the lawn.
Where the branches
bend and creak.

Branches bend and creak
With the weight of her body
Bedecked in crystal that will
soon drop to the earth,
As the branches
bend and creak.

The masquerading
beauty of winter
has come and gone
With a vengeance
we won't soon forget!

I Will Guide You With My Eye

The air was hot and dry
And a sand storm was in the making.
The antaean strength of the army
Was in pursuit of two thieves, for the taking.

The dream and birth of a plan
Unfolded in lucid detail
The army quietly moved as one man
Advancing in that sandy locale.

The thieves took a respite from running
And stopped while the storm abated,
Laying down the tile of gold in each greedy hand,
Thought the thieves, the army we've evaded.

The Army kept advancing,
The sandstorm was unwinding.
Because of patience in the face of adversity
They would persevere, not fall, finding-

The sage guidance of God...
"I will guide you with my eye," said the Lord.
So take the thieves, they did,
With valor, experience, and the sword.

Imprints

Down at the beach in the brightest of sun,
I was watching the waves one by one.
Observing their color, so bright and blue,
And in deep places, a darker hue

The vastness, the size, puts me in awe -
Our precious God made not a flaw.
The wet sand gushes between my toes.
I look back and the footprint goes.

As things in this world come and go,
Will my work stay or leave with the flow?
It seems I so clearly hear God say,
"Child, listen closely to Me today."

"Work done with Me will last forever,
"Ages of change can touch it never.
"Trust in me, and take my hand -
We'll make imprints over the land!

In Memory

"Greater love has no one than this,
Than to lay down his life for friends."
This day is a time of reflection,
Of values on which we depend.

May all men come together
To honor the dead who gave all
In love of their fair country,
Who heeded the clarion call.

Who knows a love greater than this?
"No man," the scriptures say.
Let's pay homage to God and men
On this Memorial Day!

In Memory of Daddy

I remember your kind ways
Always thinking of others first,
With a smile upon your face
By the Spirit of God, versed.

I miss you so, dear, sweet dad,
As floods of tears run down my face,
Though your mansion's far away
In my heart you have a dear place.

A place that none other can fill
For it is reserved just for you.
You were the wind beneath my wings,
Though somehow you never knew.

My emotions run deep
Like the deepest, darkest ocean.
Just one more time to tell
My love to you through emotion.

Yet, I know Jesus is the link
Between you and I.
I'm persuaded that divine love
Will make known my heart's cry.

My comfort comes in knowing
That you are in the Jesus' hands,
And someday I will see you
Within the Father's plans.

In Memory of Man's Best Friend

They say that a dog
is man's best friend and how
true that must be!
God loaned him to us for awhile,
so every little dog
has a purpose in life.
For you see, he is never
upset with with his Master
even when the Master is flying apart!
He tucks his tail between his legs,
and with his pleading eyes,
very humbly, and in ways known
only to his Master,
he absorbs the anger until
there is no more.
When he senses the anger has passed,
his tail starts spinning like a
windmill once again, and he jumps
up and down much as a child
on a trampoline.
When anyone or anything threatens
his Master's interests,
he suddenly becomes the King
of his domain.
Again he's man's best friend!
When he has come to the end
of his life, he looks at
his Master with eyes full of love,
licks him, and closes his eyes.

Such great, accepting love he gives
totally, sacrificially.
He has finished the purpose
for which he was created.
It's as though the Creator prepared
a test for mankind—one that shows
how he will respond to one
of His smallest creatures.

Jumping to Conclusion

I know the agony of jumping to conclusion,
And realizing my thoughts were an illusion.

King of Kings

All praise and honor to Jesus our King,
Who redeemed us from our sins.
Glory, hallelujah, trumpets, too,
Let songs of triumph begin.

Let us worship the King of Kings,
He is worthy of all praise,
Let praise like a river flow forth
From our lips through all our days.

Hosanna! He reigns forever more
He sits upon the throne legally;
Our God, our sin bearer, our guide,
The King of Kings sits regally!

A baby came to us in poverty:
Now He sits high upon the throne,
Won't you be ready each day,
For very soon He'll take us home!

Loved ones gathered there to meet us
Will welcome us home, everyone.
What a happy reunion that will be,
When everyone we shall see.

How very wonderful it will be
To see Him whom we've loved so long;
Our Saviour, our King, our Beloved,
We praise you with unending song.

Land of the South

The land of the south...
Land that I love.
The red clay...
symbolic of blood
that was shed so long ago.
Southern hospitality...
still belongs to this land.
The southern drawl...
like music to my ears.
Homes in the woods...
my dreams...
became a reality
in Birmingham, Alabama.
Mild temperatures...
the land of cotton and beauty.
Azalia, Camillia, and Jasmine...
are living poetry
I long to go back...
To the land of the South...
Sweet home in...
Alabama.

Laughter
Dedicated to Nellie Donnell

Laughter is sweet medicine to the soul-
It takes away the blues, prevents being droll.
A lack of merriment makes for drought,
And the all the features form a pout.

Good laughter makes us feel at ease-
Thaws out tension, anxiety's freeze.
The one so blessed is happy indeed-
From stressful life he's completely free.

Let Me See

Let me see
the steady showers of spring
the resurrection
of crocuses and tulips,
and the coming of warmer days.

Let me see
the verdant hillsides,
the crowning flowers
blooming in profusion,
and long nights with fireflys.

Let me see
the brilliant leaves
in all their pristine glory,
as the fierce wind blows
them to the ground.

Let me see
the silent fallen dust
from angels wings
on a cold winter night
and thank You for life!

Life is a Painting (Sedoka)

Life is a painting
One puts the color on it,
Will it be gray or pastel?

It may be vibrant
With jewel tones, nice to the eye.
The choice to paint it is ours.

Life's Problems (Rictameter)

God's grace
for life's problems
is the help needed now.
Let the Lord take your hand and lead
you to the victory prepared for you.
Faith is the victory, we're told,
that opens every door
taking one to
God's grace.

Like a Child (Tyburn)

Dreaming
Scheming
Screaming
Beaming
Dreaming and scheming became her way,
Screaming and beaming on any day.

Lilacs

The beauty of flowers in a vase
Sitting there regally like purple majesty
Their fragrance fills the house
Leaving their signature, you see.

Love (Senryu)

Give me one to love
As long as he's loveable.
Is this the real love?

Love is not plastic
Nor is it chrome or the like,
Love is self giving.

Devoted to love,
my earnest desire in life,
Oh, how weak I am.

Love's Quest

Give me one that I can know,
As deep as deep can be,
As God's deepest waters go,
This one and I will be.

For we'll fathom the depths together
And climb the heights of boundless love.
We'll keep our hearts for each other
As pure as a little dove.

Love's Strong Pull

Sleep my precious one
After the weary work of day.
Dream sweet dreams of fun
In paradise far away.

Rest your weary head,
Breathe alluring depths of slumber,
Sleep awile upon your bed
And leave your struggles in number.

I love you so, my heart is full
As I gaze upon your face.
I feel your love's strong pull
In this sacred, hallowed place.

But let your weary frame
Inhale the flow of peace divine,
For few hours will soon proclaim
The start of another incline.

Majestic Hills

As I lift my eyes unto the hills,
I feel such wonder and awe.
It lingers with me still -
So majestic, without a flaw.

Her lush and lofty trees
reach higher and higher till
They stand on toes to please
Their Maker, sustainer of hills.

As I look unto the hills,
From whence cometh my help?
My heart rejoices and thrills,
As My help cometh from God.

Mama

It was just like you
To stay awake 'till two,
To check my burning brow,
Then rise at dawn, somehow.

It was just like you
To do without something new,
When my eyes were wide with glee
For clothes made just for me.

It was just like you
To step aside, you knew
My little circle had grown;
I wasn't yours alone.

It was just like you
When my world had fallen through,
To be right by my side,
And ease the pain inside.

It's just like you
For the story isn't through...
Our lives go on,
Mama, I love you!

Marital Love

Marital love will thrive
If in the depths is friendship,
For it will be alive
With the two of these in kinship.

The wedding of friendship and love
Creates a happy pair
That fits just like a glove
And makes for pleasant wear.

The foundation must yet go deeper
In Christ, the solid rock,
For love must have a keeper
To keep secure the lock.

Memories of My Love

So torn and sad I felt that day
As my willow was cut down.
It was a branch planted to stay
Ever in that piece of ground.

It was in it's adolesence
Growing by spurts every year,
And as I gazed upon it once,
I was seized with awful fear.

What if lightening should strike
This graceful tree of mine,
But I cast it aside like
One would an ominous sign.

The time came when it had to go,
And that day I had to face
That never again would it blow
Around our homestead place.

It brought memories of the time
My love was taken away
While he was in his prime
On that sad and lonely day.

But the spirit came to me
In consolation, oh, so real,
As I made my earnest plea
That my aching heart he'd heal.

He brought new joy in living,
And put a song in my heart.
My Savior is always giving,
And never will depart.

Yes, He's real, so real today,
And He watches o'er His own.
He comes to them on days so gray
To bind their hearts that mourn.

Mercy

Tiny crystals
from heaven
descend as the
the rain of mercy,
and come as succor
during the arrid
times of the soul.

Micky Rooney (Clerihew)

Mickey Rooney
Is no George Clooney
But he's quite appealing
Married eight times is revealing.

.

Molds

Putting others in one's own mold
Gets a control on them, a mighty hold.

The sensitive soul feels the death like grip.
Should he resist or abandon ship?

Wanting to please he considers long,
Should he compromise, would that be wrong?

He thinks it through, decision is made,
He'll stand by it because he prayed.

God made us all in a different mold;
Some are shy and some are bold.

Each one precious and so unique;
One is quiet, while one must speak.

If we all thought alike, life would be boring,
Be no place for adventurous soaring.

We must fly in the currents of God's command
And be ourselves just the way He planned.

More Than These

"Do you love me more than these"?
I heard my Master say,
In words so warm and kind
And in a knowing way.

And as I thought upon His words,
My heart was pierced inside.
Do I love Him more than these;
Oh, could my heart decide?

As my thoughts remained on Him
Who loved me through the years,
My answer quickly came
In spite of awful fears.

Yes, I love you more than these
Because of what you've done.
Precious One, who loved me first,
My fearful heart you've won.

I'll give of what I have
To ease life's pain and pierce the dark,
Join my Jesus hand in hand
And make a mighty mark.

Godly Mother

She is filled with joy as no other,
Yet, a woman of suffering, that is Mother.

Music in a Park

Tall trees sway to the music
of Credence Clearwater and AC/DC.
The tempo of motorboats
Hum as they skip a beat
In the glassy water.
Teen's (cars with motors syncopating)
Drive where children
Play in harmony.
The light of trailers and tents
Will soon be darkened for the night,
As thunder crescendos in the hollow.

My Prayer for You

My prayer is for you today
May there be healing and health.
Always for you, I'll pray.

Spiritual wealth if I may,
And a life of joy is
My prayer is for you today.

Strength and blessings for today
From His heart of love,
Always for you, I'll pray.

Fulness and peace, I pray.
And days full of glory is
My prayer for you today.

For protection this day
In all the things that you do,
Always for you, I'll pray.

In my heart, you'll always stay
For God has put you there.
My prayer is for you today.
Always for you, I'll pray.

My Secret Garden

Rose velvet petals cozy up
to the warmth of long summer days.
The beauty is entrancing as
I meditate on the scene in a hammock,
Dreaming of the Secret Garden
of my heart.

Nature's Storm

It is dark outside
And a storm is raging.
Rain pelts the house
With herculean tears.
The lightening cracks
And streaks across the sky,
Making its presence known,
And the rolling of thunder
Brings to mind one who
Cannot be comforted.
She brings forth her offspring,
With shrieking and deep wailing.
The rain drenches the earth,
She is made to drink of anguish,
And the wind bends the
Tree with antaean strength.
Though bent, yet not broken.
The time of pain has gone.
Weep no more for the birth
has been completed,
And you will forget.
Now is the time of joy!

Never (pliades)

Nothing new under the sun
Now or forever more.
None can contend with God
Neither do away with His Word,
No, not one will dispute the Almighty.
Night has no compass and men
Need God's Word.

No Ordinary Creature

Her world of tranquility is gone;
Snatched away before she could speak or reason.
Hot tears stream down her innocent face,
as she strives to understand her terrible plight.

She tosses her head in defiance,
and the beautiful creature becomes a—wild thing.
Her large eyes narrow with determination,
as rage rises up in great tumult.

No ordinary creature is this one,
for deep in her being lies a seed of greatness,
and when anger has run it's course,
this one will be the victor – this child of divorce.

Observing Nature

How pleasant it is to get outside,
Free as a bird in spaces wide.

To feel the warm breeze upon my face,
What a day, what a place!

I see the beauty in God's green earth,
The middle of March has just given birth.

The birds are chirping and flying around.
Little daffodils peep through the ground.

The gracious willows are greening up,
With color overnight, seems strange, so abrupt.

With beauty all around it's hard to see
The weeds coming up trying to be free.

As April comes with all her showers,
Weeds form clumps like little flowers.

I must destroy them before they grow,
For into the grass their tentacles will go.

As I observe nature, I learn a lot.
Our christian lives are like this,I thought.

The weeds of sin that grow within
Mar the beauty of Christ in men.

Ode to the Village Christmas Tree

It
stands tall
With a star at the top
Depicting the star that the
Shepherds saw on that glorious
Night. It must be the most handsome
Of all the evergreen trees in the deepest woods
Angels adorn the tree depicting the angelic visitor
That brought good tidings of great joy which would be to
All people. Savior born on this day…Jesus Christ is His Name.
Pointing to God's Son on this special, wonderful and glorious day
The tree draws the community together as the lights are sparkling so.
The lights depict that one true light who said,"I am the light of
the world.
Jesus
Christ,
God in
The flesh.

Old Joe

In the south there is one called Old Joe Bonz
Who can be heard telling his tales of old
That day he began rehearsing his woes
Of sorrow, citing when he lost all his gold.

As he spoke his emotions played a part,
For he wept great tears of regret and pain.
Old Joe had been out drinkin' at the start
When he lost his gold, for he wasn't sane.

The town had heard of old Joe's bad luck
On that day when he awoke, sick of heart,
Down in the pigpen that was filled with muck.
Lo, his gold was in the muck from the start.

Old Joe learned a lesson he'd not soon forget
For his picture appeared in the Gazette!

Ordinary People

The world was turned upside down by ordinary people,
Who moved as God called and created a ripple;
The ripple became a wave that swept o'er the land;
It was living christianity led by God's hand.

God's love was burned into their hearts without measure;
It had to be shared, this precious, wonderous treasure.
So beautiful were the feet that were gospel shod,
As each one was empowered by the Spirit of God.

As then, misery, hunger, and despair reign on planet earth.
Yes, many dying souls need the new birth.
Deception covers the land like a thick, black cloud,
As humanism sits on the throne, bold and proud.

"We're living in the "New Age," men reply boldly,
While their God's are materialism and greed,
Eyes are blinded, but worship proceeds from need.
Little do they know they're without God wholly.

Abortion on demand is the law of the land.
Seldom do decent people take a stand.
The underlying theme is one of apathy,
While the baby's end is in a backstreet alley.

It will be reversed by ordinary people
Who move as God calls and create a ripple…
Ripple becomes a wave that sweeps o'er the land
It's living christianity led by God's hand

God's love is burned into their hearts without measure.
It has to be shared, this precious, wonderful treasure
So beautiful are the feet that are gospel shod
As each one is empowered by the Spirit of God.

Oh, people of God, let's go out and share the Good News.
Love demands we take it beyond our churches pews.
Just as they were called, to us He's also calling -
We've time to think it through, but no time for stalling.

Orphans

So many have been left orphans
In the world today.
Do we understand their plight
When evil men do prey?

Wake up to the devilry
Of a world filled with greed
The innocent of the race
Will languish until they are freed.

Sex rings will rule the day
And orphans will be exploited
Diabolical men waiting to pounce
From Shri Lanka to Detroit.

Evil men will wax worse and worse
Deceiving and being deceived,
Turning their ears from truth,
From holy things not perceived.

The day will come when God's mercy
Is wrapped up into conclusion.
What a joyful day that will be
For all not in delusion.

Peace Is

Peace passes all understanding,
For man cannot create it;
It descends as a golden mist,
When the mind is stayed on Christ.

Peace is composure
When death enters my world.
Peace is quiet and rest,
When I could be anxious.

Peace is flying,
When I could be crashing.
Peace is trusting,
When I could be doubting.

Peace is boldness,
when I could be paralyzed with fear.
Peace is falling asleep
In the midst of a storm.

Peace is assurance,
For death is not the end.
Peace is Jesus,
For he is the Prince of Peace!

Peaceful Valley

A feeling of peace fills
the valley.
Women come to the local village
in their freshly ironed clothes
to do business.
Yesteryear seems to transend time.
In the distance
the mountains watch
over the peaceful valley,
creating a storybook scene.
Suddenly, the clouds
blacken and are pregnant
with the promise of rain.
People head for cover
as the pregnant clouds give birth.
The smell of the wet earth
brings delight to the senses.
Verdant trees weep
their crystal tears as the
rain gains in momentum.
Just as suddenly as the clouds came,
the rain has ceased, and
Sunshine comes once again
to greet this peaceful valley.

Poetry Aflame (Triquatrain)

Poetry sublime, with meter and some to ryhme
Lines all having life in them.
Free verse speaks to the heart, it is an art.
Pouring forth t'will be a precious gem.

The Poet longs to write, though it be bright,
Or crafted in anguish of soul.
His poetry is aflame, his words he must proclaim
To speak for all who cannot, t'will be his goal.

Poo Bear (Clerihew)

His name is Winnie the Poo bear,
He's just doesn't give a care
as long as he can eat
and sit down on his seat.

Popeye (Clerihew)

Popeye never would deny
Olive Oyl when she would cry.

He taught Bluto what he should learn
When his fist, Bluto earned.

Portait of a September Sky

Painting the sky blue like the ocean,
the Artist creates a portrait.
He mixes the oils carefully and paints
golden highlights around lacy clouds.
The sun shines through,
until they are illuminated.
Beautiful white clouds are carried
by the wind into a deeper color,
majestic purple, ominous,
threatening a storm.
The rich colors the Artist chose
on the canvas are breathtaking!
The Artist has created an exquisite portrait.
Like the wind carries the clouds
into a deeper color,
I, too, am carried away in deep wonder!
To be captivated by its beauty,
lifted above earth's small realm
into heights of pleasure, is to feel
a deep sense of gratitude
to the Master Painter.

Precious Moments

We should savor every moment
For it could be our last,
And never wish away our time,
For soon it will be past.

Every season has it's beauty
For those with eyes to see,
And precious time contained within,
To treasure, not to flee.

Moments in the dead of winter
Are special as can be,
And moments in the crisis hour
Have their summoning plea.

For time will soon be past one day,
And what a price we'll pay.
We'll live with much regret
For precious moments wished away.

Proverb

Let the one who has a sudden desire for something be patient, and trust the Lord for its fulfillment, or one may spin a web that is difficult to escape.

Pruning

I thought I had mountains of knowledge,
but I had scarce fruit and lotsa foliage.
Now, I thought that things were going great,
It's good that I did not know my fate.

The pruning shears took care of me,
So that I would not become a tree.
A branch I was only meant to be...
Bearing fruit to set men free.

Rain and Snow (Double Etheree)

Rain
and snow:
God's blanket
of love to me
that gives me great joy
while I sit reading a book.
No visitors will come today
Only God and I will have this time,
When His blanket of love comes over me.
Hear the pattering on my window sill
creating a warm, cozy feeling
within my quaint little cottage.
When the snow comes this winter
It will find me waiting,
anticipating,
love on display
from my God
to me,
Yes!

Rain in Kentucky

Slowly the rain comes
down as a steady shower
Soon it pelts down in anger
As the fountain gains in power

Pouring down on the tin roof
Like wild horses running free.
While rivulets run down the pane
Stirring me, thrilling me.

There is no feeling like it
When the sky is leaden and dark
Coziness is all around
While a faint voice is heard, a lark.

Lightening streaks across the sky,
The trumpet of thunder is heard
roaring like a hungry lion,
Attacking the slowest in the herd.

The rain has subsided now
The sun comes out in its glory
The bow that God did set
Reminds me of the old story.

Reckon Your Life

Reckon your life by Sonlight,
Not by clouds of depression.
Reckon your life by smiles,
Not by the unseemly frowns.
REMEMBER THE GOD
OF THE RAINBOW,
Reckon your life by promises,
Not by fears galore.

Rejection

There's a pain that hurts deep inside,
The pain of love rejected.
There's no place to go from it,
No dark place to hide.

Jesus felt this way when rejected,
Aching deeply for mankind,
He had done nothing to men.
His heart was unprotected.

Oh, my Lord, did you feel as I?
Your pain was like the ocean deep
Compared to my little trickle
For all my sins, on you, were heaped.

You finished the bitter cup
Crying out in pain and anguish
Loving me with your last breath
Dying for all the languish.

Reminisce

Heavy clouds hang low
over the old cabin
in the foothills.
The black smoke in the
chimney curls upward,
until it becomes ghost-like,
and reaches it's limit.
Humidity thickens as
the aroma of ham and
fresh baked bread
is wafted through the air,
mixing with the fragrance
of petunias outside the door.
Oh, to reminisce!

Roses (Essence)

Roses are delightful,
The weeds far distasteful.

Roses and Music

The fragrance of roses
wafts over the large room,
joining a symphony of
music in the parlor
where two young lovers embrace.
The night is filled with the music
of two hearts beating as one.
Glorious is their romance
of purity and innocence,
like the first snowfall in the winter.
They vow to love one another,
and remember this night
of roses and music.

Sacrifice at Calvary

Jesus was a man born to die,
Eons ago it was ordained on high.
To become one of us was His mission,
From God to man, a divine transition.

He was fully God but fully man,
And He left His throne for the Father's plan.
Feel what He felt in the garden alone;
He agonized in prayer and He began to groan.

He sweated drops of blood, could he endure?
There was great suffering for one so pure.
He wanted His father's will, not a crown
So die, He must; for in sin, all were bought.

They whipped Him with a cat-of-nine tails, tore opem His back;
That day in history was black, so black.
Strugling under the cross, the heavy weight,
He was so tired and in such a weakened state.

Finally, He was relieved by one.
The man was unaware it was God's dear son.
No one ever loved like this man;
Hanging there bleeding, from God's presence banned.

He never did one thing wrong;
He just loved and He loved so strong.
He was tortured beyond all belief,
Not once was was there relief.

There were those who wept that day,
And some felt terrified and began to pray.
Darkness came and covered the earth,
While soldiers mocked His Kingly worth.

"Father, forgive them, they know not what they do."
Down through the ages I hear it too.
Oh, the torture as our filthy sins were laid on Him,
But worse would come in this scene so grim.

Such racking pain and agony of soul
In Jesus poor body was taking it's toll.
My God, my God, why have you forsaken me?"
The demons hovered there in glee.

When all looked hopeless and there was doubt,
Jesus was victorious and let out a shout!
It is finished!

All through the land the sky turned dark,
Our loving Saviour had left His mark.

The veil of the temple was rent in two,
And the tombs were opened and the dead in view.
The centurian was now able to see
That it was God's own Son who hung on the tree.

So they took His body to a rich man's grave,
Hewn out of a rock, a tiny cave.
On the third day the glad news came,
"He is risen," never to suffer shame.

He offers you heaven, eternal life,
Will you surrender that life of strife?
I caution you, do not turn Him away.
The hour is late, call on Him today.

Safe Harbor

When the storms of life surround you,
Let the lighthouse be your guide.
When around you the sea billows roll,
There is one who is on your side.

Jesus will be your safe harbor
While the angry waves are thrashing,
When the loud thunder crashes,
And the lightening flashes.

He will guide you through the storms
To that fair land above
Where storms are never known
And all is harmony and love.

Seasonal Beauty (Tanka)

The leaves are turning
To bright yellow and red
Strewn across the lane
Where lovers are caught up
In beauty of the season.

Seasons (Tanka)

The earth is alive,
The grass is greening on time,
The birds are singing
In melodious cadence.
Our God is alive and well.

Picnics are many
During the hot days of summer,
While the nights are filled
With twinkling stars and a breeze
And a song of gratitude.

The trees are turning
To bright yellow and red
Strewn across the lane,
Where two lovers are caught up
In beauty of the season

Silence of the snow
Keeps falling, falling, falling
Blanketing the earth
Like a sugary meringue
So delicious to the taste.

Shipwrecked

How many lives have been shipwrecked
While inadvertantly playing with sin?
How many more will it take
To appease the god of sinful men?
Just a taste of drugs, come on, baby,
We'll hit the high roads tonight,
There's nothing going to stop us now.
Deception, in this way, he delights.
Satan, the evil god of this world
Has slithered into their minds,
Taking them any time he wants
To do his bidding, they're quite blind.
He mocks them, tempting all the while
Until he's got them in his trap,
Then he abandons their poor soul
Only later, to let them face the rap!
He's shipwrecked many a poor soul
With his most flattering style,
If only they had eyes to see
And win over the Devil's wile.
Christ beckons, pleads with them tenderly;
Will they turn Him aside and shun?
He waits patiently at their heart's door.
Welcoming them home as sons.

Slavery Exists Today

He is hounded as a dog.
His demeanor is meek
out of necessity,
like the wind after a storm.
His lot is one of bitter dregs
for little hope is left.
He cries out in anguish of soul,
"Why does this happen to me?"
Day and night he cries out,
"Does anyone know
or care about my plight?"
God in heaven will hearken
to the cry of the slave,
and once again raise up deliverers
to set them free.

Smoky Mountain Home

The ribbon of road winds
up and down,
threading through lush trees.
And higher still
the ancient mountain climbs,
sprinkled with wildflowers,
while bushes of Rhododendron
and Mountain Laurel
grow untamed.
All of the forest stands on tiptoe
over all created things,
as creatures roam below.
On and on, going higher where
a mist hangs over the
mountains in the distance.
At last, a most charming sight
is in view…the little log cabin
perched on top of the summit.
A sentinel it will be
to the verdant valley below.
Flowers bloom profusely
in a rainbow of colors.
The sunlight moves ever so slowly
enveloping the cabin
in dappled sunlight.
Night falls with a fat moon
and blinking stars
over the little cabin
in the Smokies.

Snowman (Monorhyme)

The children play in the snow
With faces all aglow.
They'll make a snowman just so,
Where the blustery wind doesn't blow,
And where the sun isn't a foe.
A scarf around his neck will flow,
Buttons all in a straight row.
His round face looks like dough,
With a carrot stick nose to show.
His top hat makes him look in the "know."
Cranberries for a mouth, oh!
Until his mouth was eaten by a doe.

Springtime in Kentucky

My soul soars in the springtime of the year.
with wings that mount up to heaven.
Overnight the showers come to bathe
The earth in an ethereal atmosphere.

The canopy which covers the sky
With a luminescent like hue
Is a phenomenon of spring
Which only the few will view.

The transporting of spirit and soul
When flowering trees burst into bloom
And the most magnificent beauty
Of thoroughbreds skipping over knowls.

Forsythias turning a bright gold
Bringing sunlight and days of cheer
The hope of all things that are born anew
As the springtime unfolds here.

Lilacs fill the air with perfume
The sweet smelling honeysuckles
Make the fragrance overwhelming
At spring time In Kentucky, my home.

Summer (Nonet)

Oh, come quickly summer with your long
days of sipping cool lemonade
in the shade of the birch tree,
where little birds warble
and squirrels galore
are amusing,
yes, summer
is my
dream.

Summer Defined (Pliades)

Sweltering heat with
Savage weather,
Swimsuits donned,
Swimming refreshes.
Stormy skies bring
Showers of rain,
So the cycle begins again.

Sunrise

The sun has risen and the tops of the trees
Are alight with the glory of God.
The shadows are nowhere to be seen,
And the host of heaven applauds.

The sky is painted with golden hues
Mixed over folds of purple light
Changing into the brightness of day
Creating a glorious sight.

A fresh new day has once again dawned
Bathed clean in splendor and brilliance
Like the sun in the heavens
We, too, will rise with resilence.

The Beauty of Snow

The winter snow comes silently
in the night to blanket Gods creation.
Awaking to the splendor of a winter
morn is breathtaking,
it's hushed beauty—enchanting.
The sun peeps out from the gray sky,
creating a scene that sparkles with diamonds.
Crabapples—dried up—prunelike,
blanketed with heavenly snow -
laden down—hiding their features
under tiny puffs of frigid, thick cotton.
In time, spring says they must go.
The little greek maiden on the lawn
wears a pillbox hat of ermine in olden style,
as she overlooks the pool for fish.
Chairs left out from warmer days
are adorned with white,
fluffy pillows – so inviting.
A hazy gray like film envelopes
the atmosphere—making it
the thing from which dreams are made.

The Beauty of Words

Oh, the beauty of words
so sublime
that steal the breath away,
descriptive in their
uncommon utterance,
full of blissful
and poetic thoughts.

Let the bards fashion
heavenly words
that enrapture the soul
and delight the senses,
always praising the Creator
with their whole heart!

The Birds and Bees

The wonder of it all
Puts my soul in awe.
The love that's in the air
Between this lovely pair.

His plumage is bright
So beautiful to the eye
As he begins this rite
With his might he will try.

He sings a love song
As crooning, sweet and long.
Soon he'll have her eye…
By his nature, comes nigh.

The wonder of it all-
The Creator's master plan
To propagate when He calls
All creatures in the land.

The Creator of All Things

The melody of a stream babbling
over rocks sets my heart to dancing.
The cadence is harmony in the music
of nature. The warbling of cardinals
enhances the beauty of the moment.
Every now and again the breeze
leaves it's signature upon the tall grasses-
leaving just as quickly as it came.
White butterflies wing their way as
guided by the Creator of all things.
The most profound of all His works
is the human spirit who, when enlightened
by the Spirit of God,
recognizes that apart from Him
he would be a lifeless shell of a human.

The Figment of My Imagination

At dusk the clouds
in the distance-
purple and blue hues-
high above the valley-
Enrapture my senses!
Seeping into the
the figment of my imagination-
not seen-
are mountains, quite magnificent.
The mountains I have created
in my inventiveness
will regrettably disappear
when the day is over.

The Greatness of God

God created a beautiful earth,
And I am filled with awe and praise!
The rich colors stagger my mind
As the sun casts brilliant rays.

He made a carpet of emerald green,
And a ceiling of brightest blue.
He formed all of His creation
With grandeur and lofty view.

Oh, the beauty of mountains, so grand,
That slope to valleys below,
Where rivers roam o'er the land
That wisdom planned so long ago.

The great seas heed His command,
And the proud waves are stayed.
"This far shall ye go and no farther."
Was the decree He firmly made.

Once again His greatness is seen
In the starry sky above.
His power and majesty command
Our awe, our praise and love.

The Holocaust

The horror that the Jew lived with
Was a nightmare and was not a myth.

David's star, they wore on their sleeve
Knowing not, who to believe.

They were tracked like animals
By Hitler's cannibals.

The cattle cars had a heavy load
Not knowing to death, they rode.

Little children, women, and men
Over this hatred would never win.

Some of them were hanged,
Others were beaten and banged.

Still others faced the ovens
As dastardly men were rovin'.

Their hope was all but gone
From night until the early dawn.

Man learned from history, they say,
Hindsight is better today.

When will man ever learn
To Jesus Christ, they must turn.

The Knight (Triolet)

The armour of the knight was bright
As he brandished his sword in air,
Chivalrous, using all his might,
The armour of the knight was bright.
He swept up the maiden quite light.
She swooned within his manly arms.
The armour of the knight was bright
To rescue damsels, oh, so fair.

The Light of Life

And God said, "Let there be light."
And His strong Word became
Shafts piercing the darkness of night,
Setting the world aflame.

As our earth turns from the sun,
Darkness covers the land;
Another day is over and done,
Never again at our command.

Likewise, men may turn from the light,
And walk in darkness of sin,
Walking and stumbling in the night,
Missing the life that could have been.

The Mention of His Name

My heart sings at the
mention of His name.
Such a deep and
placid lake is He.
I must needs go
to the depths,
to know deep
calling unto deep,
as thunder calls
out to the lightening,
A place of peace and rest
as only Jesus can give.

The Old Pub (Limerick)

The old pub of my childhood days
was frequented by men always.
They came and stayed to get a swig,
not long until they were doing a jig,
Soon they knew drinking never pays.

The Plague

One by one, they each fell by the way
No one could help them on this day
The plague had come and it had won
They each fell by the way, one by one!

What suffering to behold, this day
Barely holding the sickness at bay
So long ago, it had been foretold
This day, what suffering to behold!

The Sentinel

A fat breasted robin
Sits atop the grape arbor;
Her head turns from side to side,
Though she has safe harber.

She watches o'er her young ones
Who attempt to try their wings;
Seeing the world for the first time;
The little vertebrates sing.

Since God made the birds to sing,
How much more should be our song
Of trust and praise to our King
With the heavenly throng!

Like the bird, God observes
From a lofty height,
As we try our wings in this world,
We'll trust in His unseen might.

The Tryst (Cinquain)

Trysting
A rendezvous
Lonely, quite desperate
Missing one another greatly
meeting.

The Wind

The leaves sway gracefully
After the angry, frenzied wind.
Once again she has desisted
And enters as a friend.

The Years Hasten (Villanelle)

The years have quickly fled,
Since my babies were so tender
No longer down these paths I'll tread.

Stories to them, I read,
Telling about God's love
The years have quickly fled.

Little ones easy to be led
either for good or for evil
No longer down these paths I'll tread.

Washing and ironing were a dread.
Mundane things consumed me.
The years have quickly fled.

A short while they were spoonfed.
It seems they grew up overnight.
No longer down these paths I'll tread.

My weeping may endure for a night,
But joy comes in the morning.
The years have quickly fled.
No longer down these paths I'll tread.

They Dreamed of a Time

Certain plantation homes
Kept their secrets well hidden.
Master's affairs with female chattel
Were not told nor were they bidden.

There were whippings and beatings,
Enough to take away all hope.
They dreamed of a time
That they would more than cope.

But the eyes and ears of good men,
Were aware of the evil within,
The shameful plight of the slaves
Would gracious men rescind.

The shame of a time gone by
Will linger with us for years.
To call it a "mistake" would hide
The blood, the sweat, and the tears.

This Land of Ours

I love this land of ours;
America, the land of the free
and the home of the brave.
She's fierce in battle, but gentle in deeds,
tough when she needs to be,
but compassionate as circumstances call.

I feel pride nearly bursting my heart,
as the Star Spangled Banner is played.
When I think of the men who gave
their lives for this land,
a tear drops from my eye;
A tear of gratitude and thanksgiving.
When taps is played, I feel the breaking
dam in my soul.

I love this land of ours;
Thank you, precious Lord, for America!
May she always be free and
may her heart be purged from
sin to righteousness.

Tom and Jerry (Clerihew)

Tom was the storm after the calm
Pursuing Jerry with a bomb,
Over and over he would hear that,
Oh, "I think I saw a puddy cat!"

Trials

Some are in the midst of heavy trials.
They are being tried by the devil's wiles.
He's cleverly raking them over the coals,
To steal their joy is one of His goals.

We must know and resist his schemes,
And set our eyes on heavenly things,
If we fight the battle and take our stand,
We can give others a helping hand.

You see that's what trials are all about.
It just makes me want to jump and shout!
God has vindicated Himself of all evil
Brought on by the devil's upheaval!

The devil comes to steal, kill, destroy…
Jesus came that we might have joy.
He showed us what God is like.
Resist Satan when he strikes.

Sometimes he strikes with disease
The vibrant, healthy one to seize.
To know good from evil, we must learn
To resist the god of this world and turn.

"Fear not," for God is on our side
He will always be our guide…
We are in the midst of an onslaught
Go forth now armed with this thought.

Truth

Comparing scripture
With scripture
is
conveying the voice
of God's
truth.

Vengeance

The pregnant air is leaping
With intrigue,
a harbinger
of the evil to come.
Each demon masquerades
as a man,
a bitter man
destined to die.
His dark plans
are those of a murderer
in the black
night of deception.
The heady emotion of hatred
is in the air…hatred
bred by jealousy
over the years.
The evil comes
in tumultuous waves
of overlapping
ferocious cruelty.
All is merciless
when death comes
with a vengeance.

~Terrorism is bred by hatred~

Very Soon (Haiku)

The days are shorter.
Very soon Fall will be here,
And the leaves will turn.

Visiting a Nursing Home

Her silvery hair was glistening
As she moved her head to hear,
Straining hard she was listening
To the words of love and cheer.

She was such a genteel one
And she wore a deep red dress.
Her age? Well, eighty plus some,
But really, that's just a guess.

"I like your pretty red dress."
I said to her that day,
And felt her cold hand press
My hand in a thankful way.

A talkative one was she
But she never looked my way.
She said she could barely see
The light of brightest day.

She just could barely hear
As I chatted with her there,
And I couldn't help the tears
As her soul she laid quite bare.

"What am I living for,
I can't even see or hear,
I'm just a mess and more."
She felt her logic was clear.

I thought, dear lady, don't you know
Your steadfastness is a spark
That ignites and makes a glow.
In this world that is so dark?

The coldness has left her hand
And Come into my flesh,
She pleaded, "Please come back again."
And I made my vows afresh!

Weighed Down

Some things are essential,
but the things we often think
to be necessary are the least
on God's list of importance,
known as "stuff."
We're bombarded with thoughts
Of grandiose things…
Saying they are quite innocuous.
Sad to say, we'll buy until
The river runs dry and worry about
How we will pay the bills later,
Then we'll add it to our "stuff."
We can't deny the urge
To possess just one more thing,
And we'll admire it for awhile,
Getting more and more "stuff."
We find ourselves encumbered
And weighed down by pretty baubles,
Leaving the simple things of life
To be trapped by all our "stuff."
Let us lay aside all of the "stuff."
And the sin that easily besets us,
And run with endurance
The race that is set before us.
Free us, Lord, from "stuff"!

Where Have You Gone? (Quatern)

Where have you gone, my sweet love?
Far from you, my love you'll shove?
I'm so in love with you today,
Yet you left and went far away.

Did you ever love as I did?
Where have you gone, my sweet love?
Icycles hang from within you,
Yet, to you, I'll always be true.

"Till death do us part," we said
In a covenant we were wed.
Where have you gone, my sweet love?
My heart is cooing like a dove.

Always loving you through and through…
No one will love you like I do.
But you don't love me anymore
Where have you gone, my sweet love?

White Sheets

The sky up above
like white sheets hung out to dry,
blinding to the eye.

Why Will You Halt

Why will you halt between two opinions?
If God be God, follow Him.
The world will call
To make you fall
By a certain, passing whim.

Leave forever the evil, treacherous path,
Eat not the bread of wickedness,
Nor follow the devil-
Or demons of evil.
Cover your carnal nakedness.

I have taught you wisdom,
I have led you in right paths,
Paths of Godly living,
A way of giving,
You will escape God's wrath

Don't halt between two opinions,
If God be God, follow Him
Jesus is the way
Each and every day-
In which we should not stray.

Woodland Path

The air is invigorating,
and this is a special day that
evokes memories…that are
kept alive by images.
Come walk with me
on this aged woodland path.
Just think of all the things
we will discover for ourselves,
creating once again a memory.
Without a doubt, there will be
butterflies dipping about
as they do on such days.
The fat caterpillar inches
his way along the path,
as though unaware of anyone else.
Once around the bend
we will discover dogwood trees
forming a lacy canopy that
we will walk under.
Freshly polished Rhodendron
will grace our walk.
There will be fronds of ferns
unfurling with life.
Just up ahead brilliant
rays of sunlight casts a Presence
where wildflowers of many
colors are blooming.
We'll stop
and pick a few
to remember
our lovely time together!

The hummingbird's small body
is suspended
in air as he gathers
nectar from flowers.
How very trusting he is!
It isn't hard to imagine squirrels
leaping from one
branch to another, while
wise ones
are stashing their acorns
under dead tree limbs.
Look up ahead...
there's a red fox!
Do you suppose
he's looking for Brer Rabbit?
Pleasant melodies
as the sound of little
song birds sing praises
to their Creator.
I wonder where this path goes?
Anywhere you can imagine!
Come walk with me once again
on this aged woodland path.

Words Hastily Spoken (Monotetra)

One stumbled in the night so dark
Upon his words that were so stark
When he heard the songs of a lark
In yonder park, in yonder park.

That day he became quite irate,
Fell into sin, a sorry state
The angry words screamed were so great
So sad his mate, so sad his mate.

Words for to bless and never curse,
God made man so he could converse
Always in love, not something worse.
Never to curse, never to curse.

A bridled tongue is pleasant too
A quiet spirit will be true,
The Spirit within that is new
Words so imbued, Words so imbued.

Printed in the United States
71484LV00002B/313-348

9 781424 157648